BRICK CITY

NEW YORK

First published in the United States, the United Kingdom, and Australia by Lonely Planet Global Limited
www.lonelyplanetkids.com

2018 2019 2020 2021 / 10 9 8 7 6 5 4 3 2 1

ISBN: 978-1-78701-802-0

This book was conceived, designed, and produced by
The Bright Press, an imprint of The Quarto Group
The Old Brewery
6 Blundell Street
London, N7 9BH
United Kingdom
T(0)20 7700 6700 F(0)20 7700 8066
www.quartoknows.com

Publisher: Mark Searle
Associate Publisher: Emma Bastow
Creative Director: James Evans
Art Director: Katherine Radcliffe
Managing Editor: Isheeta Mustafi
Senior Editor: Caroline Elliker
Project Editors: Alison Morris, Abi Waters
Design: JC Lanaway

Printed and bound in the UAE

MIX
Paper from
responsible sources
FSC® C004800
FSC
www.fsc.org

20
UNOFFICIAL
LEGO® PROJECTS
TO BUILD!

BRICK CITY

NEW YORK

Warren Elsmore

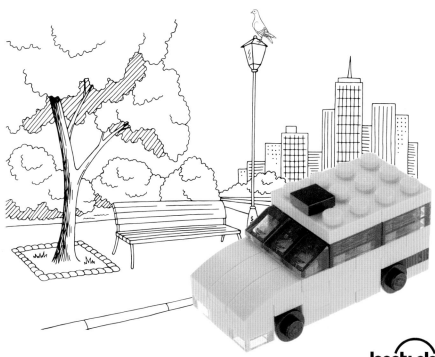

lonely planet

Contents

There are 20 projects in this book to make yourself. Just look out for the brick symbol.

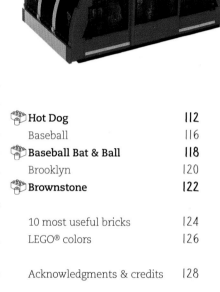

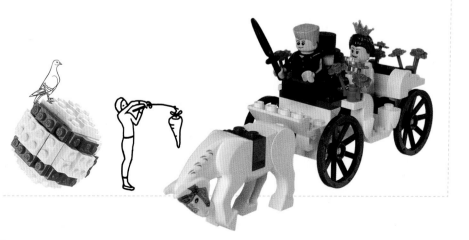

Welcome to Brick City
NEW YORK

Hey yooz! Roll up, roll up, and welcome to the most exciting city in the world—New York, New York! So good Jay Z and Alicia Keys wrote a whole song about it. Looking for a quiet life? Fuhgedaboudit!

New York City (or NYC) is big, bold, and brash. Yellow taxis honk along busy streets and steam shoots up from chimneys as shoppers jostle on the pavements.

LEARN LEGO®
BUILDING TIPS
FROM THE
PROS!

Hold the city in the palm of your hand, from a crunchy "Big Apple" to a cute mini fire hydrant. The Big Apple awaits. Go ahead and take a bite!

TURN OVER TO SEE ALL THE BUILDABLES!

Brick City New York will take you on a tour of the city's most iconic attractions, from the Empire State Building to gooey "dollar" pizza. Check out amazing LEGO® models and discover fun facts along the way. Want to know what makes Brooklyn bagels the tastiest on the globe? Or where to find a city beach? Read on...

Brick City New York includes easy-to-follow instructions for 20 unofficial LEGO® models that you can make yourself.

Brick Builds

Here's a quick visual guide to all the buildable LEGO models in this book

REMEMBER!

IF YOU SEE ME YOU CAN MAKE IT!

HOT DOG CART
PAGE 13

BIG APPLE
PAGE 18

PASTRAMI
BAGEL PAGE

YELLOW
TAXICAB PAGE 22

LIBERTY'S
TORCH PAGE 42

STEAM
CHIMNEYS
PAGE 33

STATEN ISLAND
FERRY PAGE 49

CHEESECAKE
SLICE
PAGE 56

HORSE-DRAWN
CARRIAGE PAGE 64

Macy's Parade

Macy's was founded in 1843 and its flagship
store opened in Herald Square in 1902. Every year
Macy's hosts a spectacular three-hour Thanksgiving
Parade, watched by millions on TV across the US.
Santa Claus always makes the trip to NY for the
procession. The parade is famous for its giant
helium-filled balloons—some so big they
need up to 90 balloon handlers!

**3.8 MILLION
STREET-SIDE
SPECTATORS
EACH YEAR**

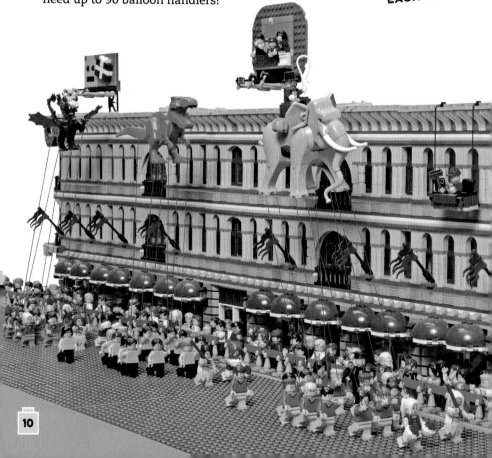

Top of the blocks

When Macy's first opened it was so far from other stores that the shop provided a wagon to ferry customers uptown. Now it takes up a whole block in what has become one of the city's busiest shopping districts.

HOT DOG CART

There is barely a New York neighborhood that does not have at least a few hot dog vendors on its street corners, although some locals would never touch one of those "dirty-water dogs," preferring the new wave of chi-chi hot dog shops all over town.

YOU CAN ALWAYS FIND A HOT DOG STAND.

YOU CAN MAKE IT!

Dogs are big business; licences for a cart in the city's most popular spots cost hundreds of thousands of dollars. Luckily this one is a bit cheaper to build.

BRICKS NEEDED

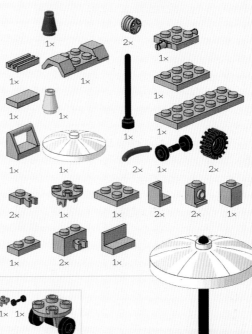

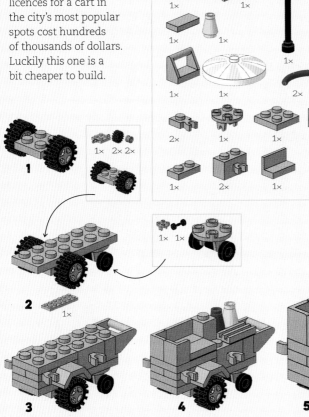

13

FLATIRON BUILDING

At 20 storeys, the wedge-shaped Flatiron was never the city's tallest building, but it soon became a much-loved New York icon. Public opinion wasn't always so positive, though. The *New-York Tribune* called it "a stingy piece of pie," while locals took bets on how far debris would spread when it blew down.

NEW YORKERS LOVE IT!

LESS THAN 6.6 FEET (2M) ACROSS

WISH YOU WERE HERE

The construction of the Flatiron coincided with the growth of mass-produced postcards. Even before it was finished, pictures were circulating the globe creating lots of excitement.

SAME SHAPE AS A SHIP'S PROW

The Big Apple

New York wears many crowns. This city is exciting to the core (geddit?) and goes by the nickname the "Big Apple." This fruity title dates back to the 1920s when a sports journalist covering the popular New York races overheard stable hands saying they were going to the "Big Apple." He used the phrase in his newspaper column and its popularity exploded from there.

A NYC fruit stand

Speaking of fruit

New York is an amazing place to eat out. The city has a surprising amount of seasonal, local food, with restaurants growing vegetables on roof gardens and embracing making everything by hand, from fancy coffee roasting to gourmet chocolate and cheese making.

WHO INVENTED THE ICE-CREAM CONE?

One of the very first pioneers was New Yorker Italo Marchiony, when he began selling ice-cream cups made from waffles bent into handy bowls.

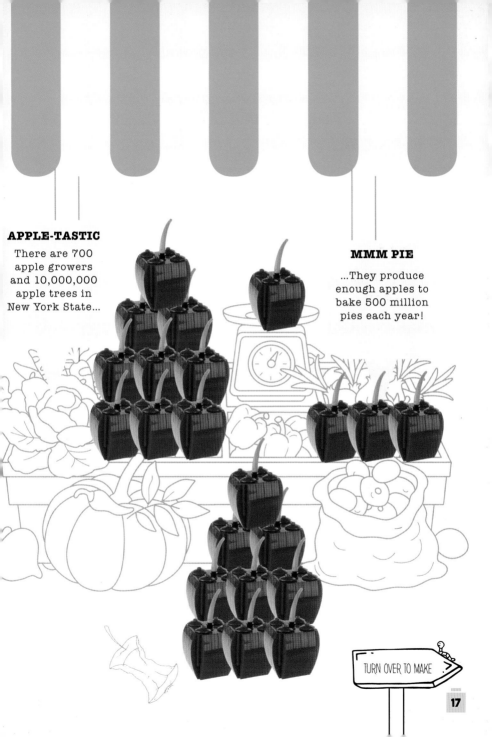

APPLE-TASTIC

There are 700 apple growers and 10,000,000 apple trees in New York State...

MMM PIE

...They produce enough apples to bake 500 million pies each year!

TURN OVER TO MAKE

Big Apple

An apple a day keeps the doctor away, and this build certainly looks good enough to eat. If you prefer your fruit to look a little less rosy try experimenting with green bricks, instead of red.

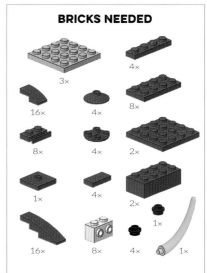

BRICKS NEEDED

3×
4×
16×
4×
8×
8×
4×
2×
1×
4×
2×
1×
16×
8×
4×
1×

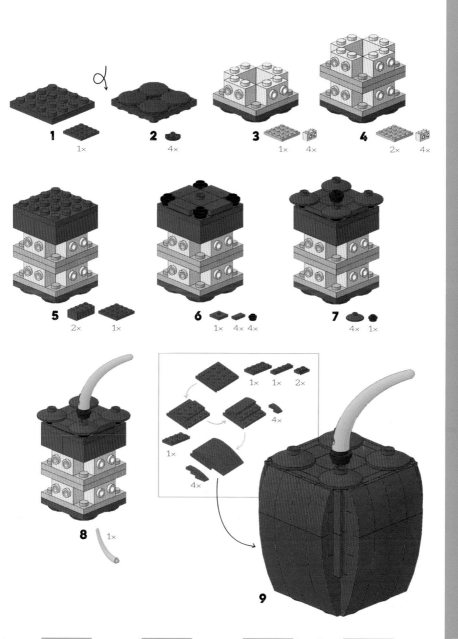

1 1×

2 4×

3 1× 4×

4 2× 4×

5 2× 1×

6 1× 4× 4×

7 4× 1×

8 1×

9

TAXICABS

When businessman Harry N. Allen was overcharged by a horse-drawn cab driver in 1907, he decided to start New York's first gasoline-powered cab service. He imported 65 red taxis from France and parked them in front of the Plaza Hotel. Later, the taxis were painted yellow after he learned that it's the color most easily seen from a distance. These taxicabs are now famed city icons.

TAXI!

Taxicabs on Brooklyn Bridge

TAXICABS IN NUMBERS

2.6 miles (4.2km) on average per trip

485,000 NYC taxi rides taken in one day

600,000 cab passengers a day

HOMEWARD BOUND

New Yorkers often complain that they can't hail a taxi between four and five in the afternoon, and there's a reason. Most cabs have two drivers and this is the time they head across Queensboro Bridge to change shifts and visit their filling stations.

TICKET TO DRIVE

Want to be a New York cab driver? First you'll need to pass a test, showing you know enough about road law and map reading. Then you'll need to pay for a medallion. There are fewer than 14,000 medallions available, and they are worth up to $1 million (£635,000).

TURN OVER TO MAKE

YELLOW TAXICAB

This cab is built from a very small number of parts. Wheels would be too large at this scale, so it uses a round plate to represent each wheel. The triangular shape of the bonnet is made using yellow slopes.

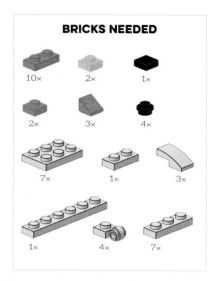

BRICKS NEEDED

10×   2×   1×

2×   3×   4×

7×   1×   3×

1×   4×   7×

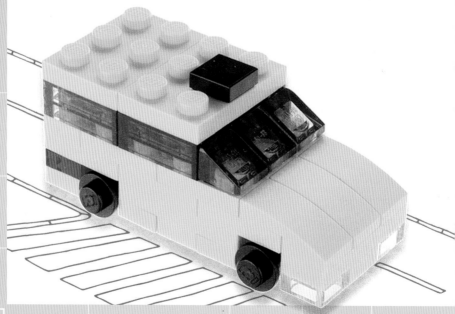

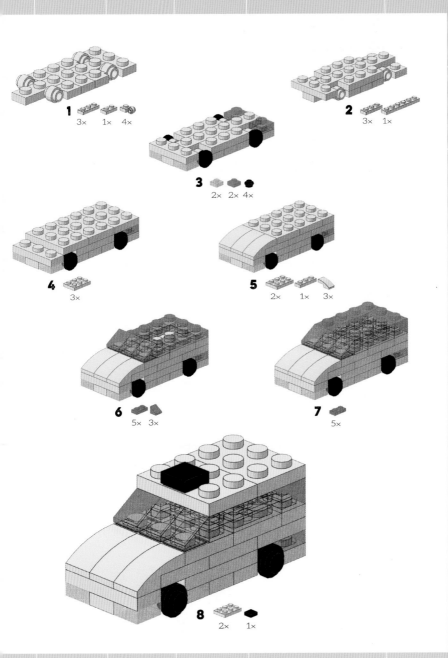

1 3× 1× 4×

2 3× 1×

3 2× 2× 4×

4 3×

5 2× 1× 3×

6 5× 3×

7 5×

8 2× 1×

Brooklyn Bridge

When the Brooklyn Bridge opened in 1883, it was the world's longest. Local people were nervous. Was it strong enough? A few days after it opened, a woman tripped down some stairs, someone cried out and soon everyone on the bridge was panicking. There was a fatal stampede and 12 people died. The following year, circus-owner P. T. Barnum led 21 elephants over the bridge to prove its strength. In fact, it's strong enough to withstand the weight of thousands of elephants.

The Brooklyn Bridge is not only popular with the thousands of people who cross it every day, it is also a hot spot for peregrine falcons. These rare birds have been found nesting there because it gives them a great view from which to hunt.

Brooklyn Bridge

THE BRIDGE IN NUMBERS

4 main cables

135 feet (41m) high

5,988 feet (1,825.4m) from end to end

THE FALCONS DIVE-BOMB FROM THE TOP AT SPEEDS OF UP TO 200 MPH (320KPH).

Delis

The word "deli" is short for "delicatessen," meaning "fine foods." German immigrants first introduced delicatessens to New York. The city is now world famous for delis from many different cultures—especially Jewish and Italian.

bun

tomato

lettuce

pickles

pastrami

mustard

bun

Brilliant Bagels

Brooklyn's bagel makers claim theirs are the best in the world due to the local water. Brooklyn's water comes all the way from the Catskill Mountains 256 miles (412km) away, and contains a special blend of minerals.

CHEFS HAVE ANALYZED THE WATER AND RECREATED ITS MINERAL MIX IN BAGELS ALL OVER AMERICA.

THE DADDY OF DELI'S

Katz's is the oldest deli in New York (1888). It serves around 9920 pounds (4,500kg) of pastrami every week. That's... well, let's just say, it's a lot of sandwiches!

Salami and pickles at Katz's

Originally from Europe, the recipe for bagels was brought to the USA by immigrants, and was once a closely guarded secret.

CRUNCHY ON THE OUTSIDE

DELICIOUSLY SOFT ON THE INSIDE

TURN OVER TO MAKE

Pastrami Bagel

Model-making is hungry work. Why not enjoy a bagel with the all the works? Pastrami, mustard, cucumber, gherkins, lettuce, tomatoes—the sky's the limit!

BRICKS NEEDED

3×

1×

10×

3×

3×

3×

1×

8×

8×

4×

9× 8×

8×

8× 8× 16×

4×

1
4×

2
3×

3
3×

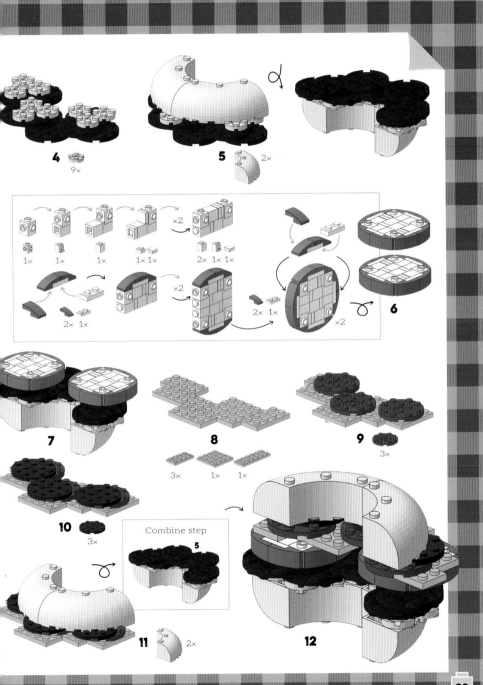

4 9×

5 2×

6

2× 1×

2× 1×

2× 1×

7

8 3× 1× 1×

9 3×

10 3×

Combine step

5

11 2×

12

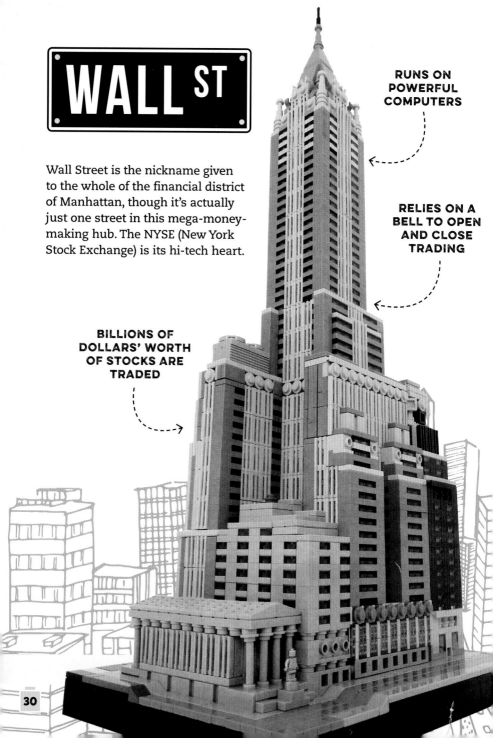

WALL ST

Wall Street is the nickname given to the whole of the financial district of Manhattan, though it's actually just one street in this mega-money-making hub. The NYSE (New York Stock Exchange) is its hi-tech heart.

RUNS ON POWERFUL COMPUTERS

RELIES ON A BELL TO OPEN AND CLOSE TRADING

BILLIONS OF DOLLARS' WORTH OF STOCKS ARE TRADED

In 1929, the US stock market collapsed during the Wall Street Crash. Afterwards the world economy sunk into the Great Depression.

Celebrities have the honor of pressing the stock exchange bell button.

Charging Bull

In 1989, a fierce-looking bull statue surprised everyone by appearing in front of the New York Stock Exchange. The artist, Arturo Di Modica, made it to symbolize US financial optimism and strength, and gave it as a Christmas present to the city. In 2017 a temporary bronze statue of a brave little girl—called *Fearless Girl*—appeared in front of the bull in a defiant pose. The bull's sculptor was not pleased.

• OCTOBER 29, 1929 IS KNOWN AS "BLACK TUESDAY" • STOCK PRICES PLUMMETED •

Steam Chimneys

Spooky wisps of steam can sometimes be seen escaping from New York's manhole covers and from striped chimneys, giving the city a haunted look at night. The steam comes from a maze of pipes that runs to 2,000 buildings from generating stations. It's used for heating, cooling, dishwashers and sterilizing hospital equipment.

Atlantic Avenue subway

On the subject of subterranean phenomena, New York's Atlantic Avenue tunnel is the world's oldest subway tunnel, built in 1844. It was built for early steam trains, which were banned from traveling through town because they had bad brakes and blew up every now and then! The tunnel closed in the 1860s. Legend has it smugglers used it to stash stolen goods and it's rumored a gangster's body was hidden down there.

YOU CAN MAKE IT!

This steam chimney is a simple, striking build. These orange and white chimneys are responsible for directing leaks above the heads of passers-by and traffic.

BRICKS NEEDED

3×   3×

1×

1

2

1×   2×

3

2×   1×

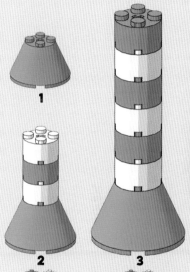

Candy-cane chimney stripes

RODENT RESIDENTS

There's one rat to every four people in NYC, but the city is spending millions on a "rat squad" of inspectors to target "rat reservoirs" and get rid of the disease-spreading furballs.

TRAFFIC LIGHTS

It's hard to believe, but until the 1920s New York had no traffic lights to speak of and policemen were stationed at crossroads to manage vehicles instead. Modern-day pedestrians are bombarded with notices, arrows, and commands, including bossy "walk" and "don't walk" signs.

PEDESTRIAN PARADISE

Foot-friendly 6$^{1}/_{2}$ Avenue offers around 0.25 miles (0.4km) of wheel-free walking. There are no traffic jams or noisy car alarms.

A busy NY street

Think like a vehicle

If you are a pedestrian on a busy NYC sidewalk, don't panic, just think of yourself as a vehicle. Follow the speed of the crowd around you and pull off to the side if you need to take out your map or umbrella. Most New Yorkers respect personal space, but they will bump into you if you get in their way!

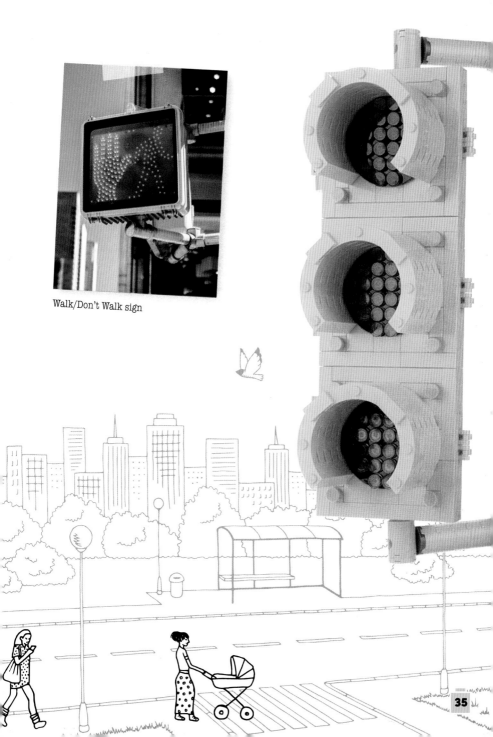

Walk/Don't Walk sign

One World Trade Center

The One World Trade Center towers above the rest of the New York skyline. The Western Hemisphere's tallest building was deliberately constructed at a height of 1,776 feet (541m). The measurement marks 1776, when the US Declaration of Independence was signed.

Also known as the "Freedom Tower."

One tower is next to the site of the original World Trade Center whose twin towers were destroyed in a terrorist attack on September 11, 2001.

A window cleaner's nightmare!

The giant pieces that make up the spire had to be delivered in the middle of the night so as not to cause chaos in the streets.

Z Z Z

THE CITY'S HIGHEST OBSERVATION DECK

73 ELEVATORS. EXPRESS ONES REACH THE TOP IN LESS THAN A MINUTE

THE TOWER IN NUMBERS

1,776 feet (541m) tall

13,000 glass panels used on the outside

22,500 cars could be made from its steel

NATIONAL SEPTEMBER 11 MEMORIAL

One World Trade Center overlooks the two huge reflective pools of the National September 11 Memorial. The pools sit within the footprints where the iconic Twin Towers once stood and the names of those who died in the terrorist attacks on that fateful day are carved into bronze panels around their edges.

BEAMS OF LIGHT

As dusk falls on September 11 each year, two powerful beams of blue light reach 4 miles (6.5km) into the sky. The Tribute in Light installation is made of 88 powerful bulbs arranged in squares that echo the shape of the Twin Towers. On a clear night, they are visible 60 miles (97km) away.

SYMBOLS OF RESILIENCE

The National September 11 Memorial Museum stands between the reflective pools. Inside, an escalator passes two giant steel beams that originally stood in the rock at the base of the North Tower. Each one is over 80 foot (24m) tall. The beams once provided the structural support that allowed the towers to soar into the sky. They stayed standing in the sea of rubble after the towers fell.

Tribute in Light

The 9/11 Memorial's reflecting pools are surrounded by 400 oak trees to represent hope and new life.

Statue of Liberty

Everyone can see that the statue carries a torch and tablet (inscribed with the date of American Independence). But what does she have at her feet? Partly hidden by clothing, there's a broken chain, representing freedom from slavery.

She stands proudly in New York Harbor and she's become a symbol of democracy. She's America's world-famous first lady of freedom: the Statue of Liberty. In fact, her full title is Liberty Enlightening the World and she was a gift to the USA from France in 1886. She represents Libertas, the Roman goddess of freedom.

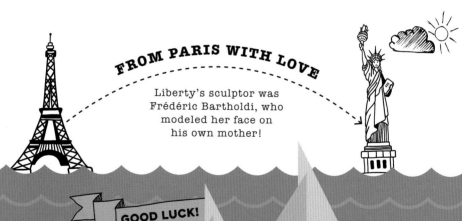

FROM PARIS WITH LOVE

Liberty's sculptor was Frédéric Bartholdi, who modeled her face on his own mother!

GOOD LUCK!

Liberty is made from over 300 parts that were shipped from France.

She needed some luck, though. The ship nearly sank in storms on the way.

LIBERTY IN NUMBERS

8 foot- (2.4m-) long index finger
25 foot- (7.62m-) long sandal
305 feet (93m) tall
154 steps inside the statue

The statue has a narrow staircase inside so that visitors can climb all the way to the crown. The crown's seven rays represent the seven seas and seven continents. It has 25 windows and if you can't visit there's a crown and a torch webcam to view online.

OUT IN ALL WEATHER

The statue's copper skin gives her inner iron frame protection, helping her to withstand the salty air of the harbor. When Hurricane Sandy hit in 2012 most of Liberty Island was submerged, but the statue was unharmed.

TURN OVER TO MAKE

Liberty's Torch

Lady Liberty is so enormous she wears size 879 shoes! Luckily this build is a tad smaller, which is useful since it involves lots of bricks.

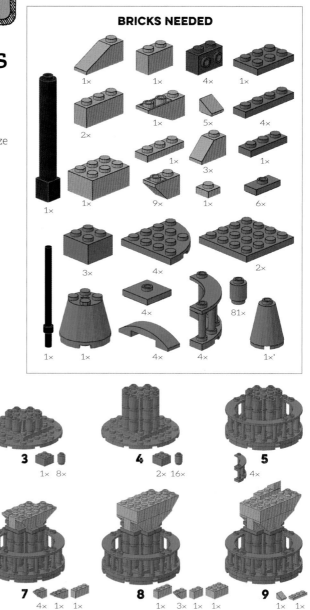

BRICKS NEEDED

1× 1× 4× 1×

2× 1× 5× 4×

1× 3× 1×

1× 9× 1× 6×

1×

3× 4× 2×

1× 4× 81×

1× 1× 4× 4× 1×

1 4×

2 1×

3 1× 8×

4 2× 16×

5 4×

6 6×

7 4× 1× 1×

8 1× 3× 1× 1×

9 1× 1×

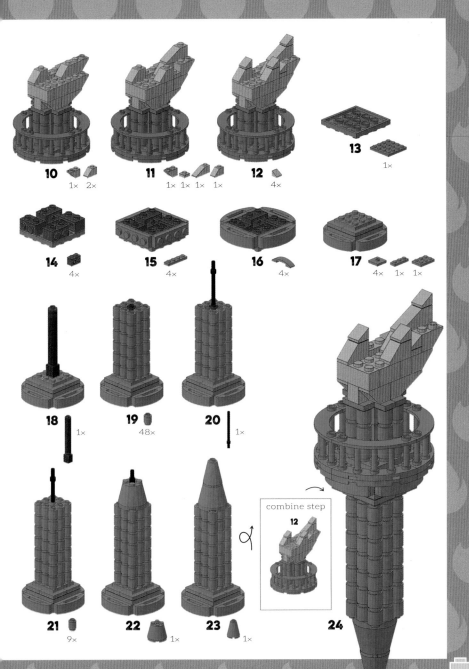

10 1× 2×

11 1× 1× 1× 1×

12 4×

13 1×

14 4×

15 4×

16 4×

17 4× 1× 1×

18 1×

19 48×

20 1×

21 9×

22 1×

23 1×

combine step
12

24

BROOKFIELD PLACE

In the heart of New York's Financial District, Brookfield Place is a seriously fancy office and shopping mall complex that sits next to the Hudson River.

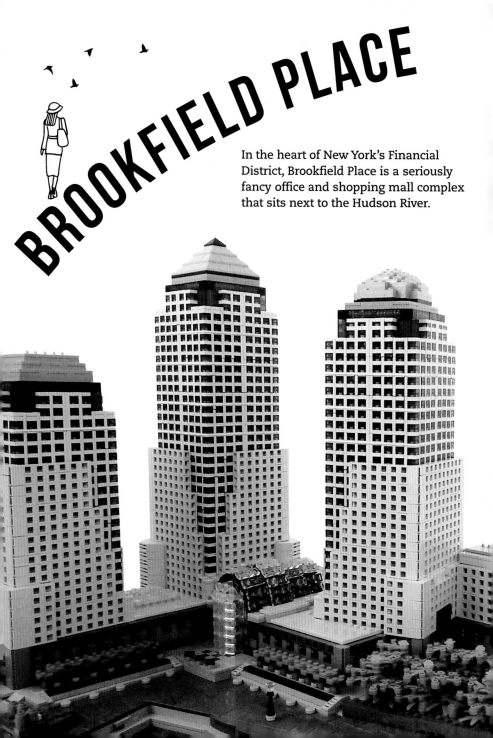

THE PAVILION

The "front door" is a glowing glass pavilion with two woven steel "basket" columns that have tree-like branches to support the roof.

The Pavilion is beautifully lit

Foodie heaven

This isn't your typical American mall, though. There are two fabulous food halls inside. French-loving foodies can hit Le District, where counters sell everything from stinky cheese to *steak-frites* (steak and chips) and savory crêpes (yummy thin pancakes). The other food hall has fancy marble counter tops and floor-to-ceiling windows.

Brookfield Place hosts lots of cool events. Pull up a deckchair and enjoy a free movie under the indoor palm trees or head to the ice rink.

ROOSEVELT ISLAND TRAM

Built in 1976, the Roosevelt Island Tram was a temporary means of transporting people to and from Manhattan until the subway station was completed. But when the subway finally opened, the tram had become too popular to close down.

TRASH TUBES

You won't find many garbage trucks in the Roosevelt Island part of town. That's because it has its own hidden garbage-sucking secret called the AVAC—a system of pipes running under all the high-rise buildings. When residents throw their garbage down the chutes, air valves suck it through underground tubes and it shoots at up to 60 mph (96.5kph) to the northern corner of the island where it gets packed into containers.

The tram takes just over 4 minutes

UNUSUAL PASSENGERS

Marvel Comics' famous superhero Spider-Man is a New York boy. His alter ego, Peter Parker, was born in Queens and lived in Forest Hills. The 2002 movie featured a thrilling scene where Spider-Man's enemy, the Green Goblin, holds people hostage on the Roosevelt Island Tram.

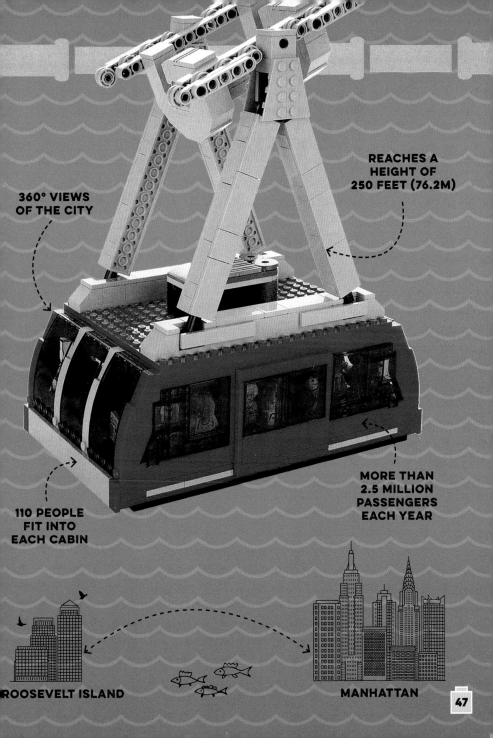

360° VIEWS
OF THE CITY

REACHES A
HEIGHT OF
250 FEET (76.2M)

110 PEOPLE
FIT INTO
EACH CABIN

MORE THAN
2.5 MILLION
PASSENGERS
EACH YEAR

ROOSEVELT ISLAND

MANHATTAN

Staten Island Ferry

The only way to get to Staten Island—southwest of Manhattan—is over the bridge in Brooklyn or on the free ferry that runs from Lower Manhattan. Around 65,000 passengers a day use the ferry. Once on the Island, visitors can go to Sailors' Snug Harbor on the north shore. It's now a cultural center with peaceful gardens, but it got its name because it was once a home for "old, decrepit, and worn-out" sailors. They don't sound decrepit, though. They were once known for their fighting!

The boats are bright orange

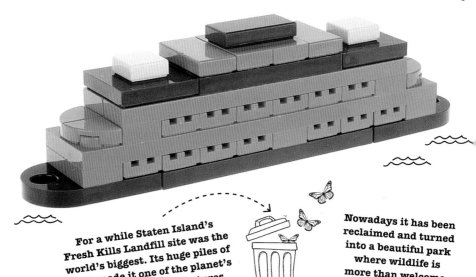

For a while Staten Island's Fresh Kills Landfill site was the world's biggest. Its huge piles of trash made it one of the planet's biggest man-made structures.

Nowadays it has been reclaimed and turned into a beautiful park where wildlife is more than welcome.

Before cars, the Staten Island ferry also transported horses back and forth! This free ferry is a city icon and you can make your own orange vessel with just a few bricks.

BRICKS NEEDED

2×   5×   13×   2×

1×   2×   2×   4×

1×   2×

1×

1×

1×

1×

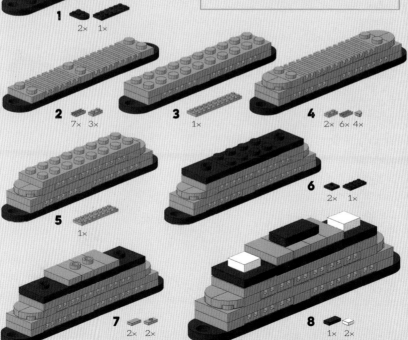

1   2× 1×

2   7× 3×

3   1×

4   2× 6× 4×

5   1×

6   2× 1×

7   2× 2×

8   1× 2×

EMPIRE STATE BUILDING

One of the world's most famous landmarks, the Empire State Building is so tall it regularly gets struck by lightning!

Luckily the skyscraper has been fitted with a lightning rod so that there's no chance of anyone coming to harm during storms.

> **LIGHTNING STRIKES AN AVERAGE OF 23 TIMES A YEAR!**

> If you ever want a fitness challenge, the ESB hosts an annual race up its 1,576 steps!

The tower has a lucky lightning rod

THE EMPIRE STATE IN NUMBERS

410 days to build

1,453 feet (443m) high

6,400 glass windows

10 million bricks in total

Pretty in lights

Since 1976, the building's top 30 floors have been floodlit in a spectrum of colors each night, reflecting seasonal and holiday hues. Famous combos include white, red, and green for Christmas, and rainbow colors for Gay Pride weekend in June.

UP, UP, AND AWAY

The antenna was originally meant to be a mooring mast for zeppelin airships, but the *Hindenberg* disaster crash put the brakes on the plan.

LOFTY AMBITIONS

Less than a year after the Chrysler Building opened, the Empire State Building stole its crown in 1931 and became the world's tallest building for over 40 years.

OBSERVATION DECKS

Unless you're Ann Darrow (the unfortunate woman caught in King Kong's grip), heading to the top of the Empire State Building should leave you beaming.

There are two observation decks. The open-air 86th-floor deck has coin-operated binocular viewers for close-up glimpses of the metropolis in action. Further up, the enclosed 102nd-floor deck is New York's second-highest observation deck...

KING KONG

The ESB became a famous movie location when King Kong climbed up it in 1933. The scene was actually filmed on set in Hollywood though.

OOPS!

POP!

For Kong's 50th anniversary they put an inflatable gorilla on the antenna, but it sadly deflated.

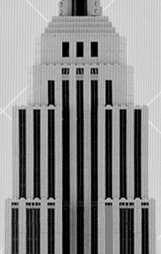

MARRY ME!

This lofty setting has featured in many romantic movie moments and is a popular spot for proposals.

YES!

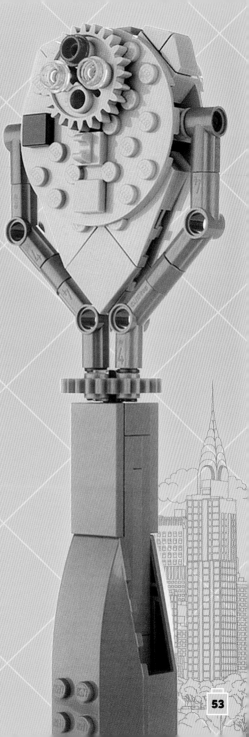

THE STAIRWAY TO HEAVEN

The views over the city's five boroughs are heavenly. They are particularly spectacular at sunset when the city wears its night-time glad rags. Some evenings the sea of lights is accompanied by a live saxophone soundtrack (requests welcome).

The viewers cost 50¢ a go

Put a grid on it

The city's amazing grid system is easy to pick out from the Observation Deck. The avenues run north to south, and the streets run east to west. The numbers start from the corner of 1st street and 1st avenue. They get higher to the west and north. Everything is the opposite in Queens.

Cheesecake

cream cheese

cream

lemon juice

vanilla

eggs

sugar

fresh fruit

New York's obsession with cheesecake began in 1921 with Leo Lindemann. His deli was the first to serve a cake that blended cream cheese, cream, a dash of vanilla, and a crunchy cookie crust. Yum! Today, New York cheesecake is a signature dish around the world.

In 1872, a farmer in Chester, New York, created cream cheese while experimenting with milk.

Cue the cheesecake revolution!

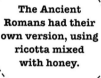

The Ancient Romans had their own version, using ricotta mixed with honey.

CRUNCHY BASE

butter

biscuit

sugar

The cream cheese version we know and love today has a crispy cookie base.

New York foodies say Junior's Deli sells the best slices—aged for 48 hours before serving

WHAT A WHOPPER!

The record for the world's largest cheesecake was created on September 21, 2013 in New York City. It weighed 6900 pounds (3129kg) and was 2 feet 7 inches (0.79m) tall.

LET THEM EAT CAKE!

WOW!

TURN OVER TO MAKE

Cheesecake Slice

America's National Cheesecake Day is July 30. Put the date in your diary and celebrate with this tasty-looking model.

BRICKS NEEDED

1× 1× 7× 3× 3×

6× 2× 2× 3× 1×

7× 1×

2× 3×

1× 4× 6×

1× 6×

4×

YUM!

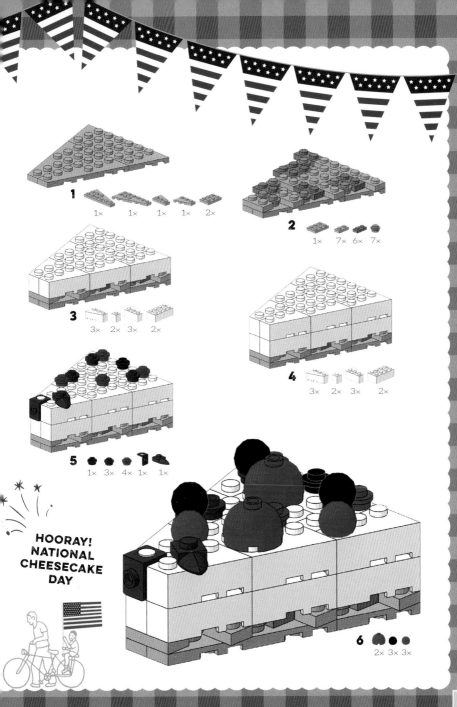

1 1× 1× 1× 1× 2×

2 1× 7× 6× 7×

3 3× 2× 3× 2×

4 3× 2× 3× 2×

5 1× 3× 4× 1× 1×

6 2× 3× 3×

HOORAY!
NATIONAL
CHEESECAKE
DAY

57

Central Park

In a city full of skyscraper-shaded streets, sometimes the sun can barely hit the sidewalk. Central Park provides a much needed escape from the concrete jungle. The park is huge, with 58 miles (93km) of paths winding through lawns, trees, and lakes. There's even a castle, a reservoir, and a zoo nestled among the greenery. It's been a nature haven for over 150 years. Around 37.5 million people visit every year...making it the busiest city park in the whole of the US.

MUSICAL MENAGERIE

Did you know there's a corner of the park where a hippo plays the violin and a penguin plays the drums? They're models on the musical Delacorte Clock in the Central Park Zoo. When the clock chimes, the animals dance to nursery rhymes, including a bear playing a tambourine, a kangaroo playing a horn, and an elephant with an accordion!

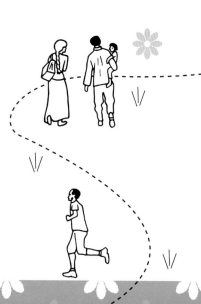

Movie moments

Hundreds of movies have been shot here, with visits from *Spider-Man*, *Men in Black*, *Godzilla*, *The Smurfs*, and *Stuart Little*, among others. The animals in the film *Madagascar* lived here, at the Central Park Zoo, before they escaped.

A walk on the wild side

All sorts of creatures live in Central Park, including beetles, spiders, bats, and owls—but the biggest surprise was a brand-new species of centipede discovered here in 2002. Ten of the mini 82-legged critters were found, and, at around 0.4 inches (10.3mm) long, they turned out to be the smallest centipedes in the world! It's thought they may have arrived from Asia in some plants.

CENTRAL PARK IN NUMBERS

7 bodies of water

36 bridges and arches

1,600 local people moved off the land to build the park

25,000 number of trees

FURRY HEROES & HEROINES

There are 29 sculptures in the park, including the likeness of Alaskan doggie hero, Balto. In 1925 he led a team of huskies over 990 miles (1,600km) from the city of Anchorage to the town of Nome, carrying a vital serum that prevented people dying in an outbreak of diphtheria.

Swampy beginnings

Wealthy New Yorkers lobbied to have the park built as a place to ride their carriages, and because they thought it would encourage people out of the town's saloon bars. The location was chosen because the land there was covered in swamps and rocks and was difficult to build on.

TURTLE REFUGE

Baby turtles make cute pets, but they're often abandoned when they grow to full size. Some have been dumped in Central Park and they've found a home in a small pool, now named Turtle Pond. Their new residence has everything they need. An island keeps them and their eggs safe from predators and offers plenty of prime sunbathing spots, too.

THE GREENEST SPOT IN THE CITY!

An aerial view of the park

Horse-Drawn Carriage

Horse-drawn carriages have been part of Central Park since the 1880s, when New Yorkers would take a ride through the park to escape the city streets. Now they're a major tourist attraction, but they're also very controversial.

Cruelty controversy

Some say it's cruel to use working horses in a city. Others say not. It's a big NYC issue, with everyone having their say about the city's resident horses.

Perfect for fans of all things horsey, Jane's Carousel features 48 beautiful hand-carved horses. Made nearly 100 years ago, it now gives rides in Brooklyn Bridge Park. These days, the carousel is enclosed in a glass box, which helped to save it when Hurricane Sandy hit Brooklyn in 2012.

New York City's working horses have at least five weeks holiday and four veterinary inspections a year.

Ride around Central Park in style

350 CARRIAGE DRIVERS

OVER 200 WORKING HORSES

TURN OVER TO MAKE

Horse-Drawn Carriage

It's hard to believe that once upon a time everyone in New York got around by horse-drawn carriage. You can make your very own using these instructions. Now you just need to figure out what to call your trusty steed.

BRICKS NEEDED

1× 1× 6× 4× 4× 4× 2×

2× 1× 2× 2× 2× 1× 1×

2× 1× 1× 1× 2×

1× 4× 1× 4× 1×

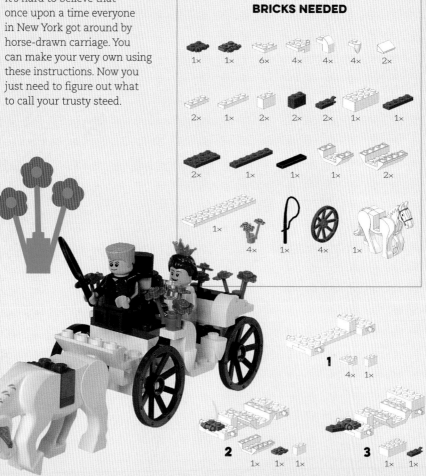

1

4× 1×

2

1× 1× 1×

3

1× 1×

Wollman Rink

Ice skating in Central Park is a quintessential New York tradition, and locals and tourists flock to Wollman Rink to soak up the magical views of the city skyline. It is a particularly special experience when the trees are frosted with snow. The rink has featured as a backdrop in many well-known films, including *Home Alone 2: Lost in New York*.

A NYC favorite since 1950

SKATING ON THIN ICE

From 1858 skaters zipped around the park's frozen lake, but from 1950 they enjoyed the more reliable ice at the Wollman Rink. It's very popular; more than 300,000 skaters sampled the ice in its first year.

GARBAGE TRUCK

They say one person's trash is another person's treasure. New York certainly produces a lot of the stuff.

Trash Museum

A garage in East Harlem is home to a secret invitation-only museum. It houses a stash of interesting trash found by Nelson Molina during his 28 years of working as a waste collector. He calls it the "Treasures in the Trash Museum," and it's a fantastic snapshot of daily stuff used around the city. Even the walls are decorated with paint found by Molina on his rounds.

HOPPER JUICE

"Hopper juice" is the smelly liquid that builds up inside the truck. Some poor person eventually has to clean it out.

YUCK!

White Elephants in New York City

PROFESSOR OF TRASH

New York University is home to Professor Robin Nagle—official anthropologist in residence to the NY Department of Sanitation—whose role is to follow garbage workers around and learn their habits.

YUM!

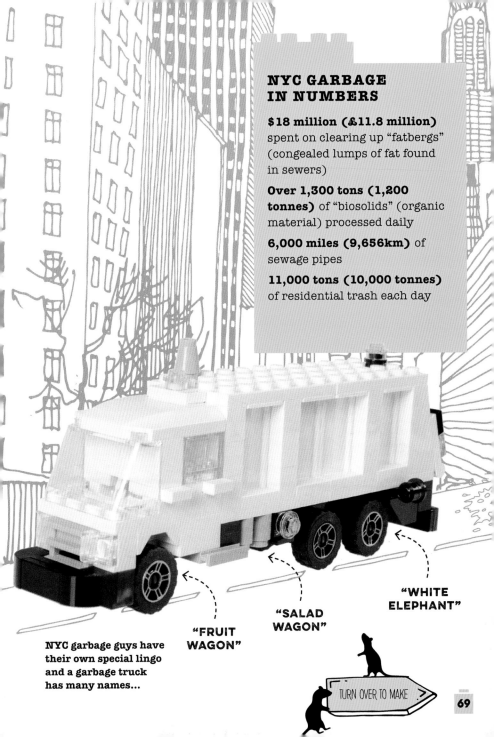

NYC GARBAGE IN NUMBERS

$18 million (£11.8 million) spent on clearing up "fatbergs" (congealed lumps of fat found in sewers)

Over 1,300 tons (1,200 tonnes) of "biosolids" (organic material) processed daily

6,000 miles (9,656km) of sewage pipes

11,000 tons (10,000 tonnes) of residential trash each day

"FRUIT WAGON"

"SALAD WAGON"

"WHITE ELEPHANT"

NYC garbage guys have their own special lingo and a garbage truck has many names...

TURN OVER TO MAKE

GARBAGE TRUCK

No hopper juice to see here! This cool garbage truck model is pristine.

BRICKS NEEDED

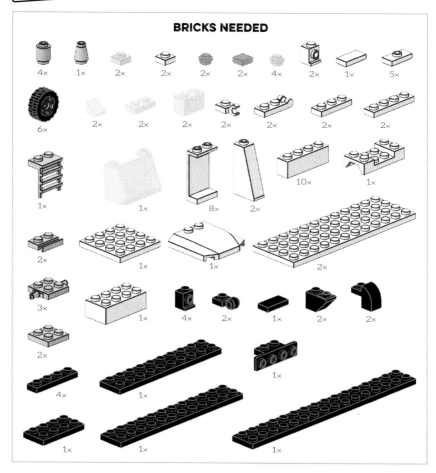

4× 1× 2× 2× 2× 2× 4× 2× 1× 5×

6× 2× 2× 2× 2× 2× 2× 2×

1× 1× 8× 2× 10× 1×

2× 1× 1× 2×

3× 1× 4× 2× 1× 2× 2×

2×

4× 1× 1×

1× 1× 1×

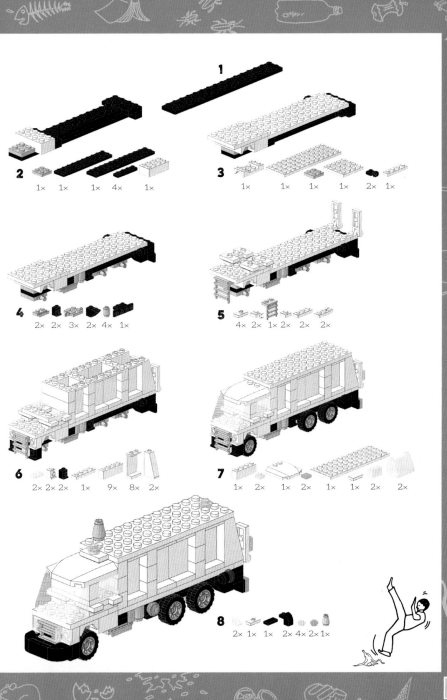

1

2 1× 1× 1× 4× 1×

3 1× 1× 1× 1× 2× 1×

4 2× 2× 3× 2× 4× 1×

5 4× 2× 1× 2× 2× 2×

6 2× 2× 2× 1× 9× 8× 2×

7 1× 2× 1× 2× 1× 1× 2× 2×

8 2× 1× 1× 2× 4× 2× 1×

HOTELS

For a city that never sleeps, New York's hotels are among the most impressive in the whole world. There are swanky joints with rooftop pools, converted factory buildings, and even a maritime-themed hotel with portholes in every room. The city's most expensive is The Ritz-Carlton—the cheapest room is a wallet-busting $995 (£736).

The Chelsea Hotel

If walls could talk, this former hotel would have many stories to tell. Famous guests included author Mark Twain, poet Dylan Thomas, artist Jackson Pollock and the singer Madonna.

The Waldorf Astoria

SECRET ENTRANCE

Deep below Grand Central is a hidden platform with an elevator to the Waldorf Astoria hotel. It was for President Franklin D. Roosevelt, who used a wheelchair. He wanted to keep his disability secret and sneak in and out unseen.

Rockefeller Center

This 22-acre "city within a city" opened at the height of the Great Depression, with developer John D. Rockefeller Jr. footing the $100 million bill. It took nine years to build, sprawling across 19 buildings with shops, entertainment, and office space. It was declared a National Landmark in 1987.

View from the Top of the Rock

An arty hub

The Rockefeller Center boasts creations by 30 famous artists. They were commissioned to make installations about a not very punchy theme: "Man at the Crossroads Looks Uncertainly but Hopefully at the Future!" The most famous have impressive titles: *Prometheus*, *Atlas* (both named after Greek gods), and *American Progress*.

TOP OF THE ROCK

30 Rockefeller (or 30 "Rock") has amazing views. You can go up to the 70th floor to sample the full "Top of the Rock" experience.

THE TOP OF THE ROCK IS 853 FEET (260M) ABOVE THE STREET!

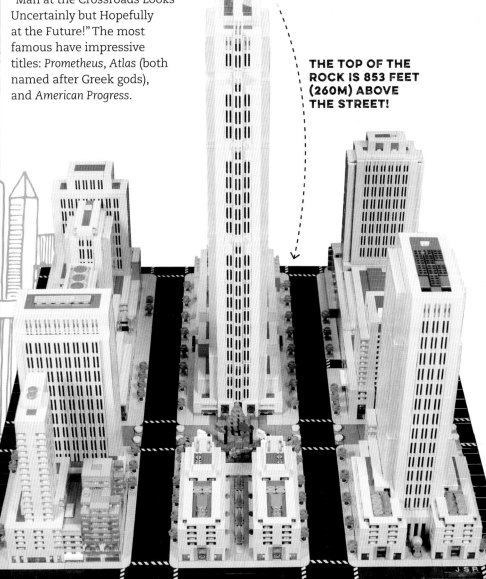

The Rockefeller
ice rink overlooked
by Prometheus and
surrounded by
the flags of the
United Nations.

Come the festive season, the Plaza is where you'll find New York's most famous Christmas tree. Lit just after Thanksgiving, it's a tradition that dates back to the 1930s, when construction workers set up a tree on the site.

Living Nativity

If you spot a camel strolling down Sixth Avenue in November or December, you're not imagining things. Along with sheep and a donkey, camels are the furry co-stars of the "Living Nativity," one of the highlights of Radio City's Christmas Spectacular stage show.

The tree is up to 100 feet (30m) tall

ICE, ICE BABY

Rink at Rockefeller Center is the city's best-known ice-skating rink.

Pizza

There are over 9,000 pizzerias in NYC and 350 slices of pizza are eaten every second across the US. There goes another 350! The whole of America celebrates the succulent slice during National Pizza Week, in January.

A slice of history

In the late 1800s, Italian immigrants from Naples brought with them their love of pizza. Gennaro Lombardi opened New York's first pizzeria in 1905, adapting his baking techniques to create the New York pizza. He catered to local tastes by cooking on coal-fired ovens and using mozzarella from cow's milk (in Naples they used buffalo milk and wood-powered ovens). We salute Gennaro for over 100 years of pizza. *Bellissimo!*

Lombardi's pizzeria

QUICK CRUST

New York prides itself on pizza with a thin crust, an even thinner layer of sauce and triangular slices. The crust can be cooked super-quickly for a city where everyone is always in a hurry.

INGREDIENTS

tomato

pepperoni

mushroom

olives

anchovy

mozzarella

pepper

HOT, GOOEY GOODNESS!

CRAZY TOPPINGS

Pizzerias offer unusual flavors in a bid to out-do each other, with toppings like cherries, squid ink, chocolate, and macaroni cheese!

TURN OVER TO MAKE >

Pizza Slice

BRICKS NEEDED

Make your own pizza pie with this colorful model. NYC has hundreds of "dollar pizza" joints, which sell cheap cheesy slices.

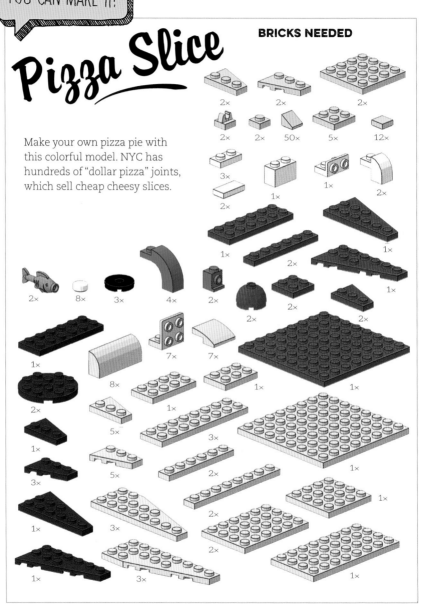

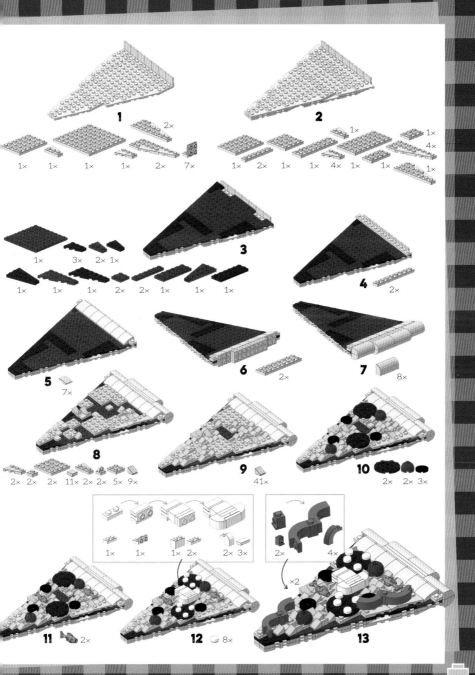

1

2× 1× 1× 1× 1× 2× 7×

2

1× 2× 1× 1× 4× 1× 1× 1× 1× 4× 1×

3

1× 3× 2× 1×

1× 1× 1× 2× 2× 1× 1× 1×

4

2×

5

7×

6

2×

7

8×

8

2× 2× 2× 11× 2× 2× 5× 9×

9

41×

10

2× 2× 3×

1× 1× 1× 2× 2× 3×

2× 4×

×2

11

2×

12

8×

13

GRAND CENTRAL TERMINAL

Completed in 1913, Grand Central Terminal is a true New York beauty. Covered with marble floors and ticket counters, its amazing main concourse has a ceiling showing the constellations. When commuters complained that the sky is backward—painted as if looking down from above, not up—they were told that it was intentional (possibly to avoid having to admit an error!).

Grand Central and The Glory of Commerce

LOST & FOUND

There have been all kinds of things left at lost and found, including false limbs, a $100,000 (£65,500) violin, and a singing President Bush doll.

Cell phones are the most common lost items.

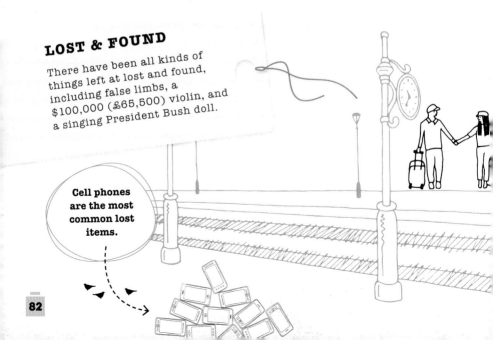

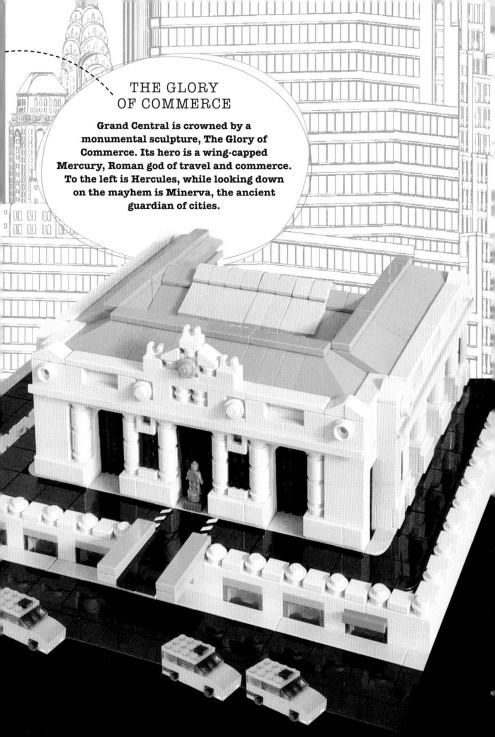

THE GLORY
OF COMMERCE

**Grand Central is crowned by a
monumental sculpture, The Glory of
Commerce. Its hero is a wing-capped
Mercury, Roman god of travel and commerce.
To the left is Hercules, while looking down
on the mayhem is Minerva, the ancient
guardian of cities.**

GRAND CENTRAL TERMINAL
CLOCK

MIND THE GLASS

Each January, a huge glass-walled squash court is set up beneath the grand chandeliers of the main waiting room for the annual Tournament of Champions. Spectators can get a close-up view of the game.

The information booth at Grand Central Terminal is said to be the most popular place to meet up in New York. You can stand there watching some of the 750,000 people who cross the concourse daily or perhaps take a look up at the clock on top of the booth, which has four faces made of opal and is worth around $10 million (£7.1 million). Staff at the booth answer 1,000 questions an hour!

TICK TOCK

SHHHHHH!

Whispering secrets is a popular habit at the Grand Central Terminal. There's an area of archways on the way down to the lower concourse where messages can be whispered to the wall and heard by someone listening at the one diagonally opposite.

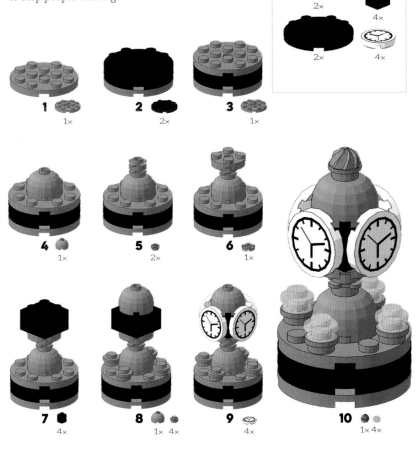

YOU CAN MAKE IT!

Never run late again with this four-faced timepiece. Grand Central has the lowest rate of passenger slip-ups in the country as the trains always leave a minute later than scheduled to stop people rushing.

BRICKS NEEDED

1× 4× 2×

2× 4× 1×

2× 4×

2× 4×

1 1×

2 2×

3 1×

4 1×

5 2×

6 1×

7 4×

8 1× 4×

9 4×

10 1× 4×

New York Public
Library

Loyally guarded by the marble lions of "Patience" and "Fortitude," New York's Public Library was the largest marble structure ever built in the US when it opened in 1911. Its Rose Main Reading Room is beautiful; many visitors get a sore neck gazing up at the fluffy clouds and cherubs on the ceiling.

MAP MANIA

The Map Division has 431,000 maps and 16,000 atlases, some dating as far back as the 16th century.

Rose Main Reading Room

Literary treasure trove

This amazing building is home to precious manuscripts by just about every famous author, including an original copy of America's Declaration of Independence and a Gutenberg *Bible*.

THE REAL WINNIE-THE-POOH

Once upon a time, a little boy called Christopher Robin Milne was given a teddy bear by his mum. Watching him play, his writer dad, A.A. Milne, got ideas for stories about the bear, named Winnie-the-Pooh. Soon the character had become world famous. The original toys now sit in a basement at the library, behind bulletproof glass.

AMERICAN MUSEUM OF NATURAL HISTORY

Famous palaeontologists Barnum Brown and Henry F. Osborn traveled the world collecting dinosaur bones, then brought them back to New York. Thanks to them, the American Museum of Natural History (AMNH) has the world's largest collection.

Dem bones

Up on the fourth floor there are more than 600 complete, or near-complete, skeletons of dinosaurs and other prehistoric reptiles and mammals. Museums often use plaster casts to replace the missing bones in incomplete skeletons. Around 85 percent of the skeletons at the AMNH are made up of real fossilized bones.

T. REX IN NUMBERS

6 inch- (15cm-) long teeth

5 foot- (1.5m-) high skull

39 feet (12m) long from nose to tail

OH HI!

HORIZONTAL MOVES

One of the most awesome skeletons is the ferocious predator Tyrannosaurus rex. Scientists once thought this hunter walked upright, but we now know that it held its body and tail horizontally.

Barosaurus

Ankylosaurus

GOOD SENSE OF SMELL

The museum's T.rex is two skeletons combined!

GREAT EYESIGHT

SHORT ARMS

SERRATED TEETH

No dino bones have ever been unearthed in New York State, but we know dinosaurs must have lived here because footprints were discovered in Rockland County.

POWERFUL LEGS TO OUTRUN PREY

Diplodocus

Triceratops

TURN OVER TO MAKE!

YOU CAN MAKE IT!

T.REX SKELETON

The American Museum of Natural History T. rex has two heads! A lightweight fake head and a real skull nearby, which is too heavy to put on top of the real bones. This tiny model dino is more of a middleweight.

BRICKS NEEDED

 1×

 1×

 1×

1×

 1×

 1×

 4×

 2×

 1×

 1×

1×

 4×

 1×

 2×

 1×

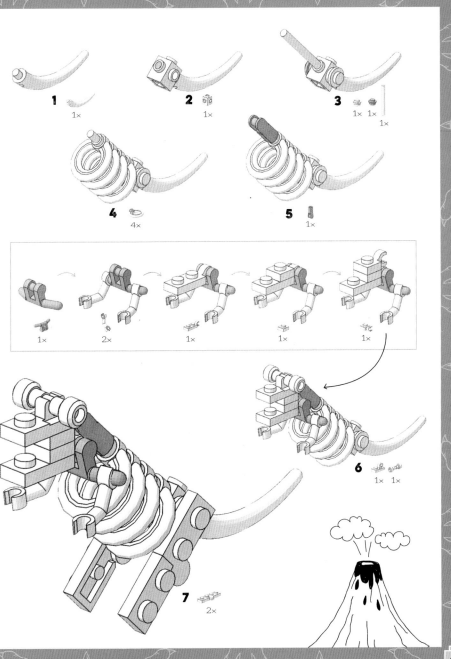

1 1×

2 1×

3 1× 1× 1×

4 4×

5 1×

1× 2× 1× 1× 1×

6 1× 1×

7 2×

Fire Hydrants

If the hydrant doesn't have a sprinkler cap the water can be strong enough to send someone flying!

Although they are officially intended for use by firefighters, New York's iconic fire hydrants are more often opened up by residents to create impromptu water features when the city swelters. Using a strong magnet and wrench the hydrants can be opened to produce a cooling, rainbow-riddled mist for local kids (and their parents).

MAGNET KEEPER

Officially you are supposed to fill in a form before you open a hydrant, but every block has an unofficial magnet person who opens and closes them.

New York's cute fire hydrants are painted different colors depending on their water pressure. You can easily make this cherry red one yourself. Just add water!

BRICKS NEEDED

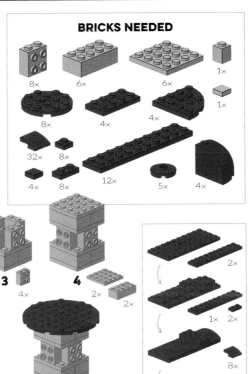

8× 6× 6× 1×
8× 4× 4× 1×
32× 8× 12× 5× 4×

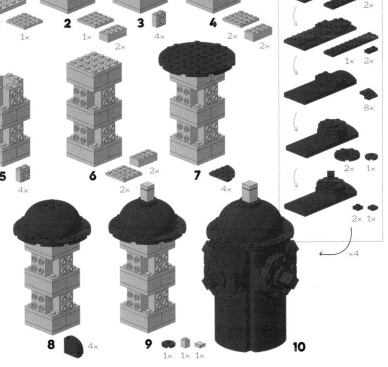

1 1×
2 1× 2×
3 4× 2×
4 2× 2×

5 4×
6 2× 2×
7 4×

2× 2×
1× 2×
8×
2× 1×
2× 1×
×4

8 4×
9 1× 1× 1×
10

THE SUBWAY

The New York subway is far more than a simple transit system, it's a citywide phenomenon. If you laid all the transit track end to end it would stretch all the way from New York to Chicago.

Going underground

NYC's subway art comes in all shapes, sizes, and styles. It includes: mosaic murals, nautical charts, quotes, photography, stained glass, and sound installations.

THE SUBWAY IN NUMBERS

14 under-river "tubes"

72 bridges

468 station stops

5.6 million daily travelers

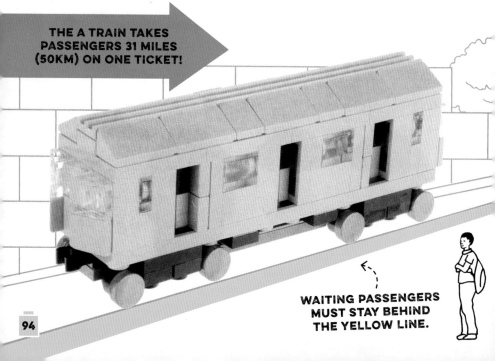

THE A TRAIN TAKES PASSENGERS 31 MILES (50KM) ON ONE TICKET!

WAITING PASSENGERS MUST STAY BEHIND THE YELLOW LINE.

TWEET, TWEET!

ART ON THE LINE

A green box suspended above the platforms at 34th Street-Herald Square allows travelers to play music while they're waiting for a train. It's an art installation called *REACH*, by Christopher Janney. Waving a hand in front of one of its "eyes" breaks a beam and triggers soothing birdsong, melodic music, or rain sounds.

LITTLE FIGURES

One of the most popular artworks is *Life Underground* by Tom Otterness at 14th St-8th Ave. His little figures pop up where you least expect them—sitting by commuters, crawling along railings, or climbing walls.

14th Street-Eighth Avenue Station

TURN OVER TO MAKE

SUBWAY TRAIN

If you're riding the NYC subway you have to be aggressive enough to push your way on before the doors close. Luckily, this model isn't quite so stressful to make.

BRICKS NEEDED

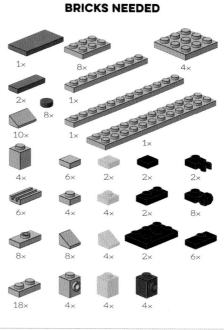

1× 8× 4×
2× 1×
8×
10× 1×
1×
4× 6× 2× 2× 2×
6× 4× 4× 2× 8×
8× 8× 4× 2× 6×
18× 4× 4× 4×

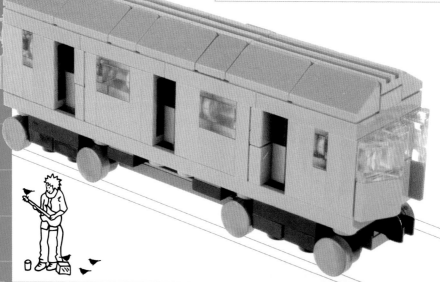

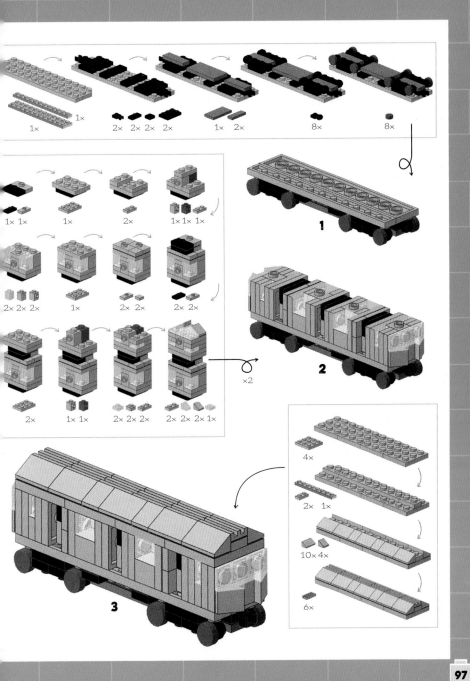

1× 1×

2× 2× 2× 2×

1× 2×

8×

8×

1

1× 1× 1×

1×

2×

1× 1× 1×

2× 2× 2×

1×

2× 2×

2× 2×

2

×2

2×

1× 1×

2× 2× 2×

2× 2× 2× 1×

3

4×

2× 1×

10× 4×

6×

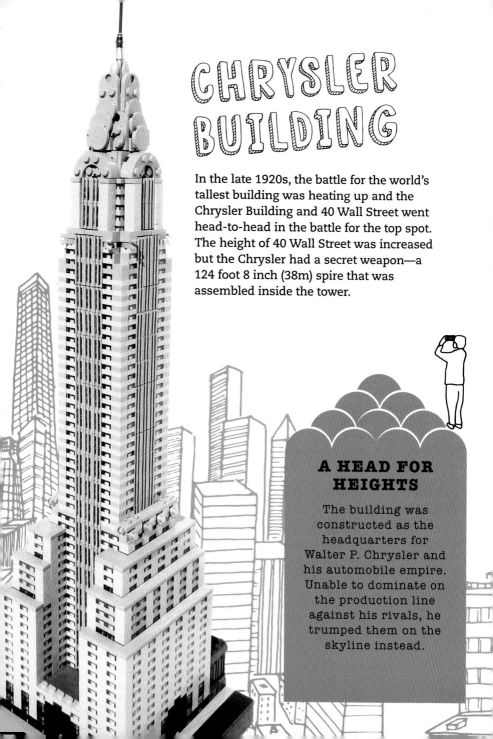

CHRYSLER BUILDING

In the late 1920s, the battle for the world's tallest building was heating up and the Chrysler Building and 40 Wall Street went head-to-head in the battle for the top spot. The height of 40 Wall Street was increased but the Chrysler had a secret weapon—a 124 foot 8 inch (38m) spire that was assembled inside the tower.

A HEAD FOR HEIGHTS

The building was constructed as the headquarters for Walter P. Chrysler and his automobile empire. Unable to dominate on the production line against his rivals, he trumped them on the skyline instead.

IMPRESSIVE SPIRE!

World's tallest...or not!

The Chrysler was world's tallest building for 11 months, until the Empire State Building was built.

DISTINCTIVE CURVES

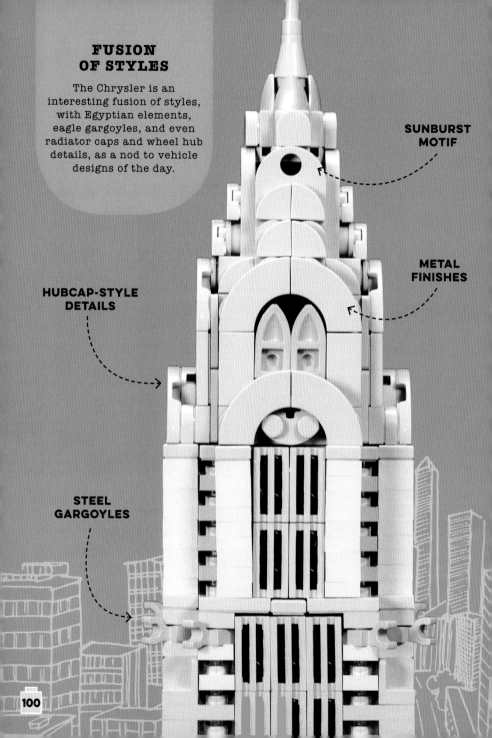

FUSION OF STYLES

The Chrysler is an interesting fusion of styles, with Egyptian elements, eagle gargoyles, and even radiator caps and wheel hub details, as a nod to vehicle designs of the day.

SUNBURST MOTIF

METAL FINISHES

HUBCAP-STYLE DETAILS

STEEL GARGOYLES

EEK!

There are 8 gargoyles on the 61st floor

AHOY THERE!

The telescopes at the top of the Empire State Building (see page 50) have the best views of the gleaming Chrysler.

Lobby loveliness

The Chrysler's lobby is one of the city's most impressive. It is decorated with the world's largest mural, at 97 by 100 feet (29.6m by 30.5m), showing buildings, aeroplanes, and busy workers on Chrysler assembly lines.

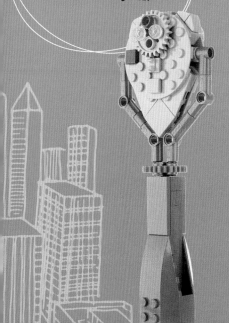

THE CHRYSLER IN NUMBERS

1,047 feet (319m) high

77 floors

2 years to build

Graffiti Spray Pain

Graffiti was born in New York—in the 1970s, graffiti-covered subway trains were an unofficial symbol of the city. Fine artists such as Jean-Michel Basquiat and Keith Haring even started including graffiti elements into their work. In the 1990s a new generation of artists (lots of them with art-school degrees) started using spray paint to make illegal art.

Who's that man?

World-famous graffiti artist Banksy came to New York in 2013 and created art all over the city for a month. The NYC police were on his tail but they never caught him!

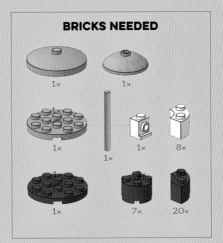

YOU CAN MAKE IT!

Spray paint is a graffiti artist's most important tool of the trade. They have to work quickly so that they don't draw too much attention. This cute graffiti spray paint can is easy to build.

BRICKS NEEDED

1×   1×

1×   1×   1×   8×

1×   7×   20×

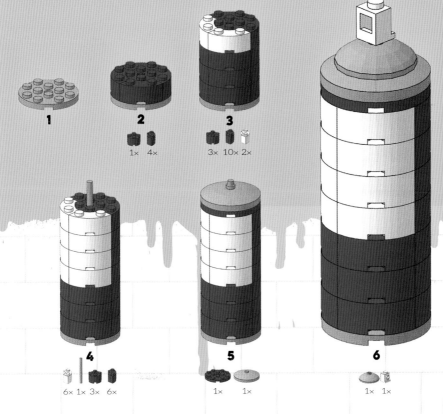

1

2
1×   4×

3
3×   10×   2×

4
6×   1×   3×   6×

5
1×   1×

6
1×   1×

A NEW PERSPECTIVE

The High Line provides a unique perspective on the city—especially at its viewpoints where panes of glass frame the streets below.

HIGH LINE

Here's a park that's perfect for a sky stroll. A favorite spot of New Yorkers, the High Line is built on a dingy, disused railway line and elevated 30 feet (9m) above the streets of Manhattan's West Side. This is a place to sit and watch the traffic go by below you, or to peek into nearby buildings if you're feeling a bit nosy.

The park provides a habitat for wildlife and is used by locals for everything from stargazing to practicing tai chi. Along the route there are lots of intriguing things to see including art installations, wide deckchairs for soaking up the sun, and a water feature for toe-paddling.

ECHINACEA FLOWERS ADD A POP OF PINK!

ALL ABOARD THE GHOST TRAIN

It's said that the High Line is haunted by ghost trains and phantom passengers. Apparitions include a cowboy who fell from the line and a mysterious person who lived beneath the tracks.

Wild & wonderful

Unlike many parks, where the plants are brought in and planted, the gardeners here welcome "volunteer" and native plants that sprout wild on the tracks.

New Yorkers soak up the sunshine

The last train to run here had two cars carrying a cargo of frozen turkeys!

On warm evenings walkers can enjoy views of the lit-up city and sparkling stars.

TURNTABLES

In 1973, a teenager called Kool Herc started hosting parties in a community room in his Bronx high-rise home. He started using two turntables to loop beats...and that, so they say, was the birth of hip hop! Lots of other sound makers have followed Kool's creative lead and there's still loads of innovative music going on in the area.

BREAK BEATS

During the 1970s there was a wave of fire attacks in the South Bronx neighborhood. They reduced many apartment blocks to cinders. Hip-hop was born from the ashes, with Herc on the decks and the Rock Steady Crew inventing athletic break dancing. Crews would "battle" each other in competitive dance-offs.

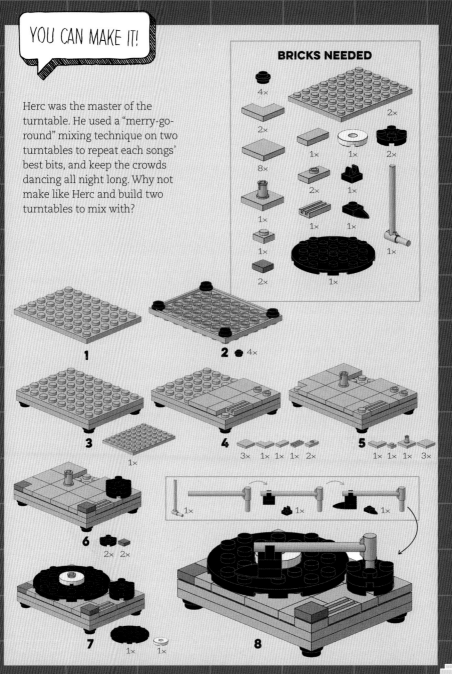

Herc was the master of the turntable. He used a "merry-go-round" mixing technique on two turntables to repeat each songs' best bits, and keep the crowds dancing all night long. Why not make like Herc and build two turntables to mix with?

BRICKS NEEDED

4×
2×
2×
1× 1× 2×
8×
2× 1×
1×
1× 1× 1×
1×
2×
1×

1

2 ● 4×

3

1×

4 3× 1× 1× 1× 2×

5 1× 1× 1× 3×

6 2× 2×

1×

7 1× 1×

8

Coney Island

Only 50 minutes by subway from the center of the city, Coney Island is a popular seaside neighborhood. The wide sandy beach has lots of nostalgic, colorful charm, with a wooden boardwalk and an amusement park with a famous roller coaster.

New Yorkers have been coming here for more than 150 years to chow on hot dogs, catch a sideshow and dress up like punk mermaids at the annual Mermaid Parade. It ain't Disney —but it isn't meant to be.

LUNA PARK

In the early days the area was pretty rough-and-ready, with a bad reputation. Luna Park was one of Coney Island's first family amusement parks. It opened in 1903—a dream world with live camels and elephants, lit by more than a million bulbs. It is still possible to ride the Wonder Wheel (opened in 1920) and clackety Cyclone roller coaster (1927).

PUCKER UP!

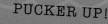

Coney Island's New York Aquarium is the oldest in the US. The sea lions put on amazing shows with their trainers, dancing and diving. They even kiss on command!

HOT DOG

Hot dogs are a New York staple. Served with sauerkraut (chopped pickled cabbage), onion sauce, ketchup, or mustard, and sold from hot dog carts.

A classic 'dog

A NEW YORK STAPLE

HOT DOGS IN NUMBERS

70 hot dogs eaten annually by the average American

20 billion hot dogs eaten at US sports events in a single year

Hot dog eating competiton

The fastest hot-dog eaters in the world converge in Coney Island every Fourth of July to compete for the honor of eating as many hot dogs as they can in 10 minutes. This all takes place in front of a crowd of 50,000 or more, plus a huge television audience. Before the competition begins, all the contestants are weighed and then arrive in front of the crowds on the "bus of champions."

Nathan's Hot Dog Eating Competition

YUM

TURN OVER TO MAKE

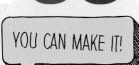

HOT DOG

No one knows for sure who invented the hot dog but you can follow in their footsteps with this fun build. Why not try yours with the works?

BRICKS NEEDED

5×
9×
2×
8×
4×
4×
8×
6×
4×
4×
1×
12×
2×

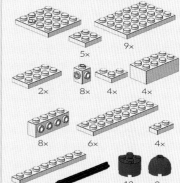

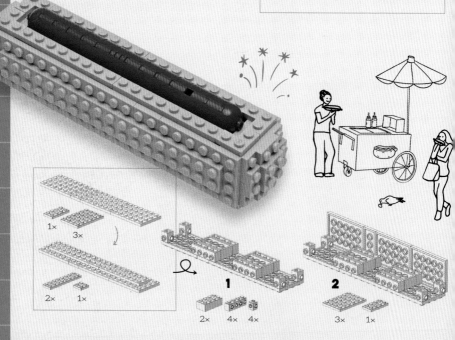

1×
3×
2×
1×

1
2×
4×
4×

2
3×
1×

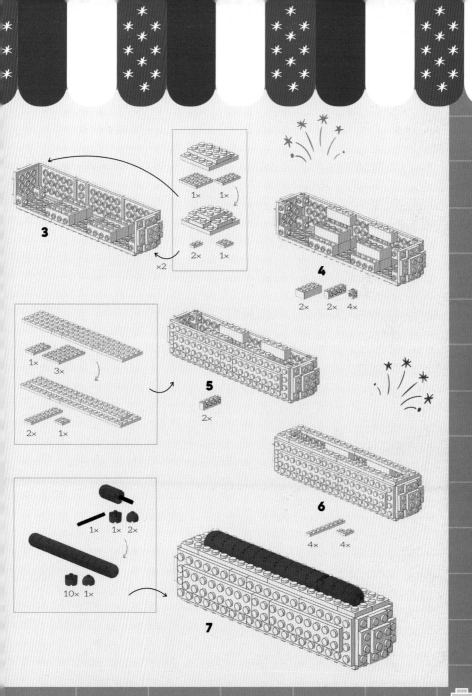

3

1× 1×

2× 1×

×2

4

2× 2× 4×

1×

3×

2× 1×

5

2×

6

4× 4×

1× 1× 2×

10× 1×

7

BASEBALL

The Yankees and the Mets are New York City's two famous baseball teams. The Yankees play at the Yankee Stadium. In 2009 they moved from the original building to a site across the street. The new stadium cost $2.3 billion (£1.5 billion) and is one of the most expensive sports venues ever built.

Jeter's House

The original 1923 stadium was nicknamed "The House That Ruth Built" after legendary player Babe Ruth. When he died in 1948, his body lay in state there and was viewed by more than 100,000 fans. The new stadium has been christened "The House That Jeter Built" after Derek Jeter, the Yankees all-time top batter, who retired in 2014.

BLEACHER CREATURES

The "Bleacher Creatures" are a group of loyal fans who always sit in the same spot and chant a roll call of the Yankees' names at the start of a game, until each player responds to the call.

The team was founded in 1901 in Baltimore, Maryland, with the name the Baltimore Orioles.

They moved to NYC in 1903 as the Highlanders, and didn't become the Yankees until 1913.

They're nicknamed "The Bronx Bombers."

Famous players include Joe DiMaggio, Mickey Mantle, and Lou Gehrig.

Field at the Yankee Stadium

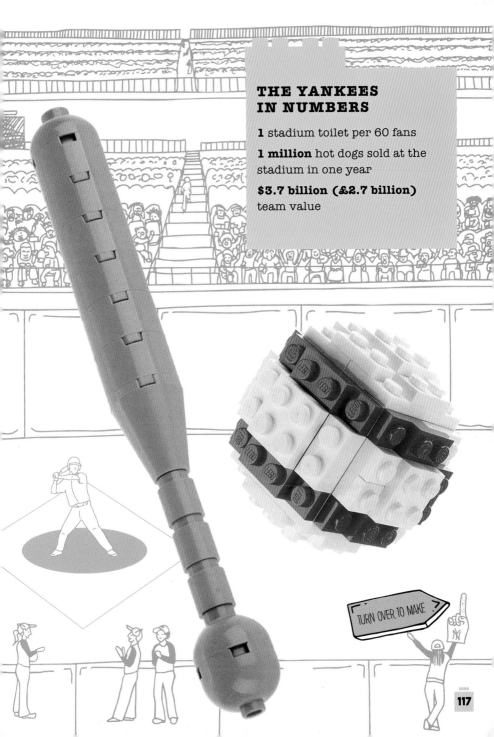

TURN OVER TO MAKE

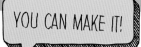

BASEBALL BAT & BALL

When the Yankees switched stadiums there was an increase in home runs. People blamed the walls for creating a wind that lifted the ball up! Here's hoping your bat and ball are just as lucky.

BUILDING THE BAT

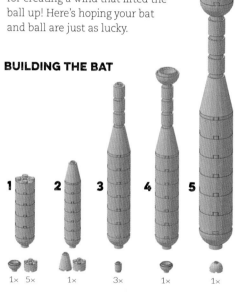

1 5× 1×

2 1×

3 3×

4 1×

5 1×

BAT BRICKS NEEDED

6× 3× 1× 2× 1×

BASEBALL BRICKS NEEDED

2× 4× 8×

3× 8×

10× 2×

10× 4× 4×

6× 1× 2×

BUILDING THE BASEBALL

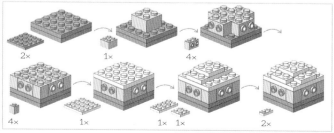

2× 1× 4×

4× 1× 1× 1× 2×

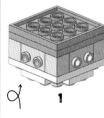

1

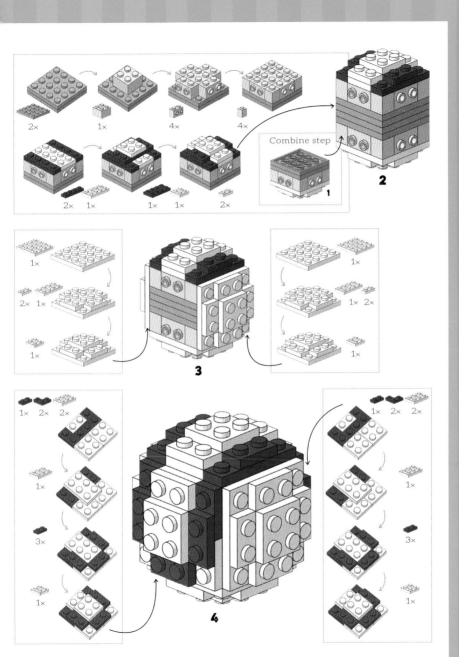

Combine step

BROOKLYN

Many Brooklyn neighborhoods are known for their handsome "brownstones." These old townhomes are separated from the street by steep staircases called stoops.

Brownstone is actually a type of sandstone and it varies in color depending where it was mined and the minerals in it. It can actually be pink, red-orange, or purple-ish, as can the buildings themselves.

HELP!

The steps are known as "stoops"

BROOKLYN SUPERHERO SUPPLY CO.

When superheroes run out of X-ray vision power or need to try out a cape in a wind tunnel they head for the Brooklyn Superhero Supply Co. Here they can buy superpowers such as magnetism or stock up on basics like antimatter.

One wealthy brownstone owner wanted a lobster tank in their property!

Stoops were designed to raise the houses above the piles of horse poo on the streets.

TURN OVER TO MAKE

YOU CAN MAKE IT!

BROWNSTONE

This brownstone model was built with the plates pointing sideways to give more detail. There are a few tricks to getting the sideways plates to attach, as you will see.

BRICKS NEEDED

1×	2×	10×	3×	8×	4×

4×	1×	2×	9×	4×	2×
					2×

1×	2×	3×	2×
2×		1×	

2×	1×	2×	2×

1×	2×	6×	2×	1×

7×	6×	1×	1×	1×

1×	1×	1×	4×	18×	19×	1×

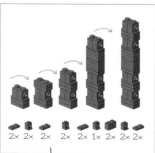

2× 2× 2×　2× 2× 1× 2× 2× 2×

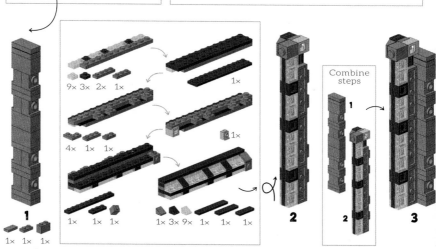

1

1× 1× 1×

9× 3× 2× 1×　　　1×

4× 1× 1×　　1×

1× 1× 1×　　1× 3× 9× 1× 1× 1×

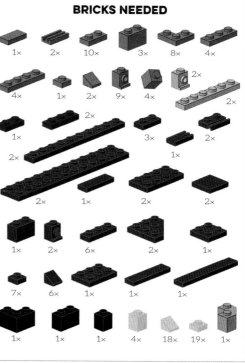

2

Combine steps

1

2

3

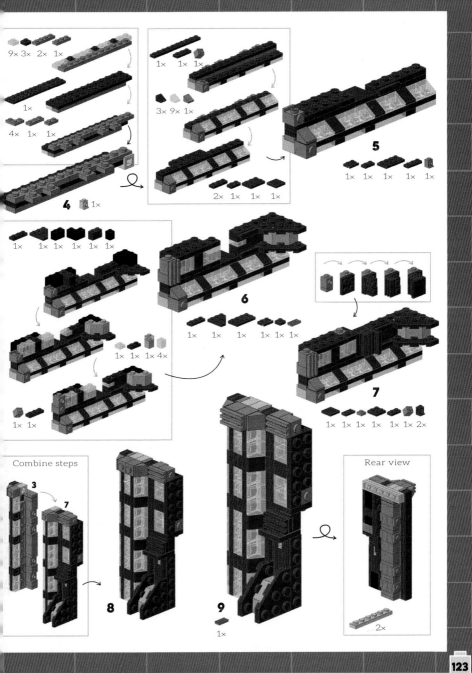

9× 3× 2× 1×

1×

4× 1× 1×

4

1×

1× 1× 1×

3× 9× 1×

2× 1× 1× 1×

5

1× 1× 1× 1× 1×

1× 1× 1× 1× 1× 1×

6

1× 1× 1× 1× 1× 1×

1× 1× 1× 4×

7

1× 1×

1× 1× 1× 1× 1× 1× 2×

Combine steps

3

7

8

9

1×

Rear view

2×

10 most useful bricks

These are the most exciting bricks in LEGO®
building. No matter how many of them you
have, there will never quite be enough!

1

2×4 BRICK

The oldest brick
around, this is a
classic. Strong, and
great for adding
structure to
something fragile.

2

1×2 BRACKET

Introduced in 2012,
and so useful! These
pieces help where
other brackets can't
and add real strength
to your models.

3

1×1×2/3 SLOPE
(or "cheese" slope)

A great piece
that gives models
a smooth, modern
look. Useful for
buildings, vehicles,
and animals.

4

1×1 ROUND PLATE
WITH HOLE

These parts
are perfect for
anchoring rods.

5

TECHNIC PIN JOINER

Structural steelwork
is very important in
architecture and
these pieces joined
together are just the
right shape.

6

1×4 PLATE HINGE

Small but strong
hinges that let you
choose the exact
angle for the pieces
of your creation.

CHEESE SLOPE

SOME REALLY USEFUL TIPS

BRICKS & PLATES

One LEGO® brick is equal in height to three LEGO® plates. Plates give models more strength (they make great floors), and can incorporate more color variety and detail in the same space as a brick (see below).

3 = 1 Brick

"SNOT"

It stands for "Studs Not On Top"—this is a method of turning bricks or plates sideways to make it possible to create quite an accurate curve by turning half of the plates sideways. (see below).

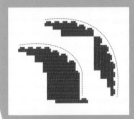

7

1×1 "HEADLIGHT" BRICK

The original "Studs Not On Top" (SNOT) brick, used for headlights on millions of cars. Its geometry is actually very clever.

8

1×1 BRICK WITH A STUD ON ONE SIDE

These bricks give you a simple way of attaching a plate to the side of a brick. They are used for details or to add a special brick in an unexpected way.

7

1×2 PLATE WITH ONE STUD

(or "jumper")

When two studs are just too much! Jumpers offset the fine details.

10

1×1 BRICK WITH STUDS ON FOUR SIDES

These are fantastic for creating columns as they can point plates out in four directions.

LEGO® colors

With more than 140 LEGO® colors to choose from, which should you use?

Not all parts exist in all colors, and in fact some very common parts have never been made in some of the obvious colors.

Below and opposite is a guide to some, but not all, of the colors available, using their Bricklink names rather than the official LEGO® ones.

DARK
PURPLE

TAN

TRANS-NEON
ORANGE

TRANS-PINK

LIGHT
YELLOW

DARK
BROWN

PINK

TRANS-BLUE

OLIVE
GREEN

PEARL
GOLD

TRANS-LIGHT
BLUE

TRANS-GREEN

CHROME
SILVER

BRIGHT LIGHT
BLUE

DARK FLESH

LIGHT
PURPLE

AQUA

HOW TO FIND THE BRICKS YOU'LL NEED

No matter how many LEGO® bricks anyone has—it's never enough! You don't need to worry if you don't have exactly the same bricks as I've used for these models though. Just try building them with the bricks you have and your imagination!

If you do need to buy more bricks to build some of the models in this book, then I've got some tips for you. Did you know you can buy bricks directly from www.lego.com? There is a special section on their online store, just for bricks. Here you can choose from a huge selection of bricks in all sorts of colors to help you build your city. If you're after something very different though, there are special websites allowing people like you to trade bricks? The two best known are www.bricklink.com and www.brickowl.com.

They work just like eBay—but for LEGO® bricks and that's where I buy lots of the bricks for my own creations.

FUN RANGE OF COLORS

TURQUOISE

SAND BLUE

PEARL LIGHT GRAY

PEARL BLACK

BRIGHT YELLOW

TRANS-RED

YELLOW

EARTH ORANGE

VIOLET

DARK RED

TRANS-PURPLE

TRANS-NEON GREEN

SAND GREEN

TRANS-DARK BLUE

TRANS-ORANGE

BRIGHT PINK

DARK BLUISH-GRAY

DARK ORANGE

TRANS-CLEAR

REDDISH BROWN

DARK TURQUOISE

TRANS-BLACK

DARK PINK

RED

PEARL SILVER

WHITE

LIGHT BLUISH-GRAY

GREEN

DARK AZURE

DARK TAN

PURPLE

MARBLED SILVER

ORANGE

MEDIUM DARK PINK

TRANS-YELLOW

BRIGHT GREEN

BLUE

LIGHT ORANGE

BRIGHT LIGHT YELLOW

DARK GREEN

LIME GREEN

DARK BLUE

MEDIUM BLUE

BLACK

MAERSK BLUE

Acknowledgments

I'd like to thank the other amazing builders who helped to contribute to this book. Spencer Rezkalla and Rocco Buttliere had already created some amazing LEGO® models of New York icons and as they say, there's no point in re-inventing the wheel! In addition, my thanks to Alastair Disley, Kirsten Bedigan, Guy Bagley, and Teresa Elsmore for being instrumental in bringing the book to life!

WE ALWAYS LIKE TO SAY THANK YOU!

Picture Credits

The publisher would like to thank the following for permission to reproduce copyright material

Alamy: p45 Clarence Holmes Photography; p54 Richard Levine; p95 Alessandra Pezzotta; p101 Eric Bechtold; p102 Nikreates.

Getty Images: p50 Predrag Vuckovic; p78 Andrew Pini.

Shutterstock.com: p16 Stuart Monk; p20 Bufflerump; p26 Leonard Zhukovsky; p33 Gary Yim; p34 Valerii Lavtushenko; p35 Andrey Bayda; p37 Jack Aiello; p38 Stockelements; p46 Drop of Light; p48 Drop of Light; p53 Aba; p61 TierneyMJ; p62 Leonard Zhukovsky; p66 MISHELLA; p68 Nielskliim; p72 Marco Rubino; p74 Ray Warren Creative; p77 Lzyllama; p78 LittlenySTOCK; p82 Photo.ua; p86 jiawangkun; 106 Pisaphotography; p112 Gabriela E. Rodrigues; p113 Elzbieta Sekowska; p116 Mike Liu; p120 Matej Kastelic.

LEGO builders: p6, 9,14 Flatiron Building, p6, 9, 36 One World Trade Center, p8, 38 National September 11 Memorial, p7, 8, 72 Rockefeller Plaza, p7, 80 Grand Central Station, p7, 9, 96 Chrysler Building ©**Spencer Rezkalla**; p6, 9, 30 Wall St, p6, 44 Brookfield Place ©**Rocco Buttliere**; p6, 9, 50 Empire State Building, p6, 56 Central Park, p7, 108 Coney Island ©**Warren Elsmore**.

Other: p7, 80 Grand Central Terminal® **Metropolitan Transportation Authority.** Used with permission.

While every effort has been made to credit photographers, The Bright Press would like to apologize should there have been any omissions or errors, and would be pleased to make the appropriate correction for future editions of the book.

ABOUT THE AUTHOR

Warren Elsmore is an artist in LEGO® bricks and a lifelong fan of LEGO®. He is based in Edinburgh, UK. He has been in love with the little bricks since the age of four and is now heavily involved in the LEGO® fan community. Since rediscovering his love of LEGO® at the age of 24, Warren has never looked back. In 2012, after 15 years in a successful IT career, he moved to working full time with LEGO® bricks and now helps many companies to realise their own dreams in plastic. He is the author of several LEGO® books and has organized several international LEGO® conventions.